Johann Sebastian Bach

Complete Concerti for Solo Keyboard and Orchestra

in Full Score

From the Bach-Gesellschaft Edition

Dover Publications, Inc.
New York

Contents

The present volume includes the seven concerti in which a solo keyboard (originally harpsichord) is the only or main soloist (BWV 1057 also features two recorders or flutes). These concerti were composed in Leipzig in the years 1735 ff., and are almost completely based on earlier extant or lost concerti by Bach for violin and/or wind instruments.

Not included in this volume are: the concerti for more than one keyboard (BWV 1060–1065); the Concerto in A Minor for flute, violin and keyboard (BWV 1044); or the fragmentary Concerto in D Minor for keyboard and oboe (BWV 1059).

This Dover edition, first published in 1985, is an unabridged republication of seven keyboard concerti from Volume (Year) 17 (slated for 1867, actually published 1869; second volume of the series *Kammermusik*, edited by Wilhelm Rust) of the set *Johann Sebastian Bach's Werke*, originally published by the Bach-Gesellschaft in Leipzig. For more information, see the detailed table of contents above, which is a new feature of the present edition.

Manufactured in the United States of America
Dover Publications, Inc., 31 East 2nd Street, Mineola, N.Y. 11501

Library of Congress Cataloging in Publication Data

Bach, Johann Sebastian, 1685–1750.
   [Concertos, harpsichord, string orchestra]
   Complete concerti for solo keyboard and orchestra in full score.

   Reprint. Originally published: Leipzig, 1869. (Johann Sebastian Bach's Werke ; v. 17).
   Contents: BWV 1052, D minor—BWV 1053, E major—BWV 1054, D major—[etc.]
   1. Concertos (Harpsichord with string orchestra)—Scores. 2. Concertos (Harpsichord)—Scores. I. Bach, Johann Sebastian, 1685–1750. Concertos, harpsichord, orchestra, BWV 1057, F major. 1985.
M1010.B24D7   1985   85-751119
ISBN 0-486-24929-8

Concerto in D Minor (BWV 1052)

Concerto in E Major (BWV 1053)

41

Allegro.

Concerto in D Major (BWV 1054)

Violino I.

Violino II.

Viola.

Continuo.

Cembalo.

Adagio e piano sempre.

Concerto in A Major (BWV 1055)

Allegro ma non tanto.

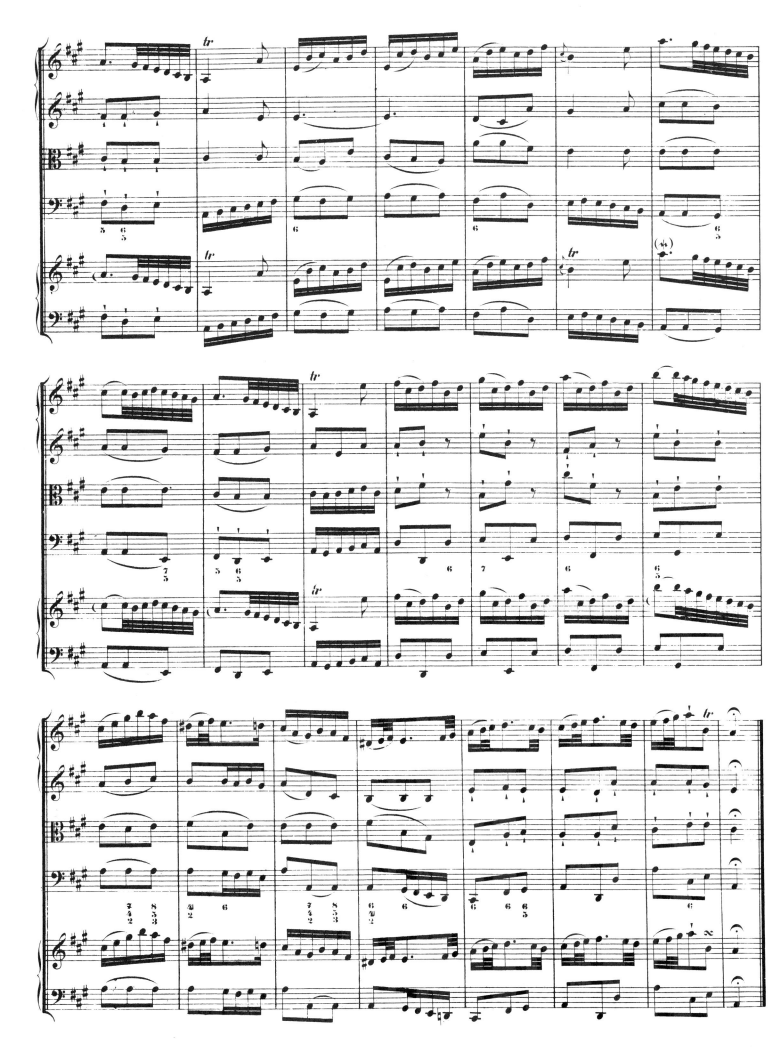

Concerto in F Minor (BWV 1056)

(forte)

Presto.

Concerto in F Major (BWV 1057)

(forte)

Violone e Violoncello.

148   Concerto in F Major

(forte)

Andante.

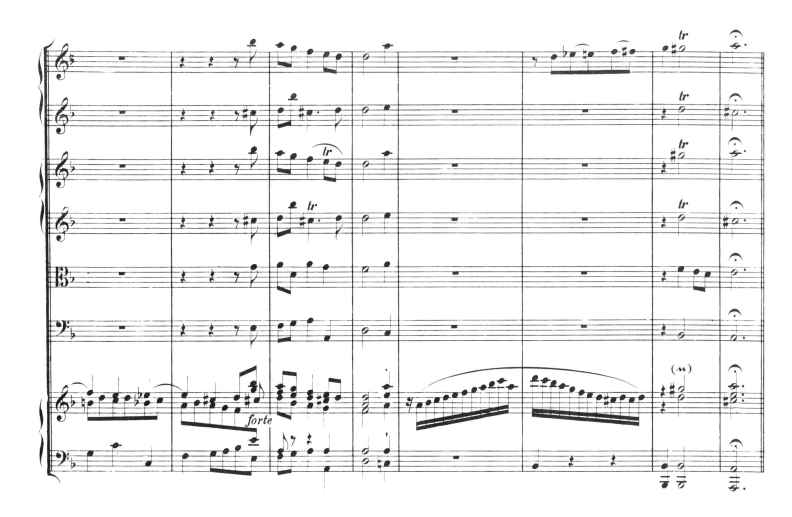

Allegro assai.

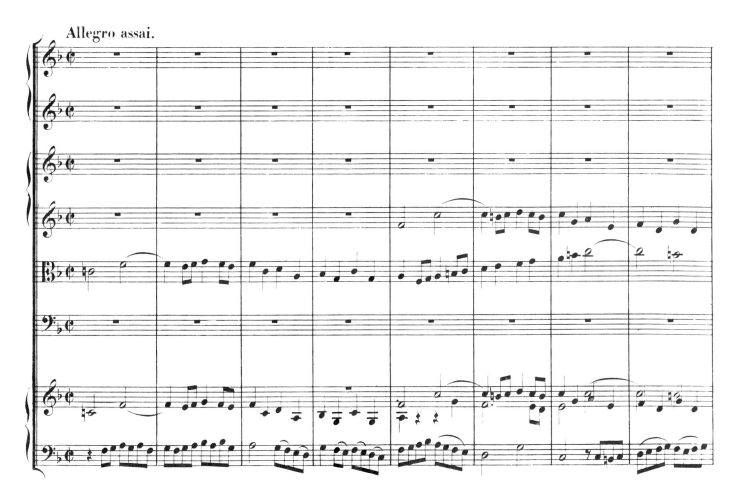

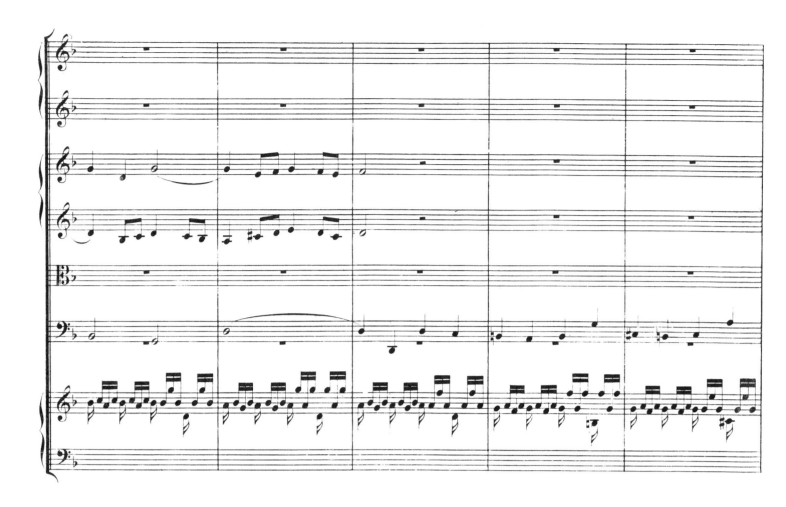

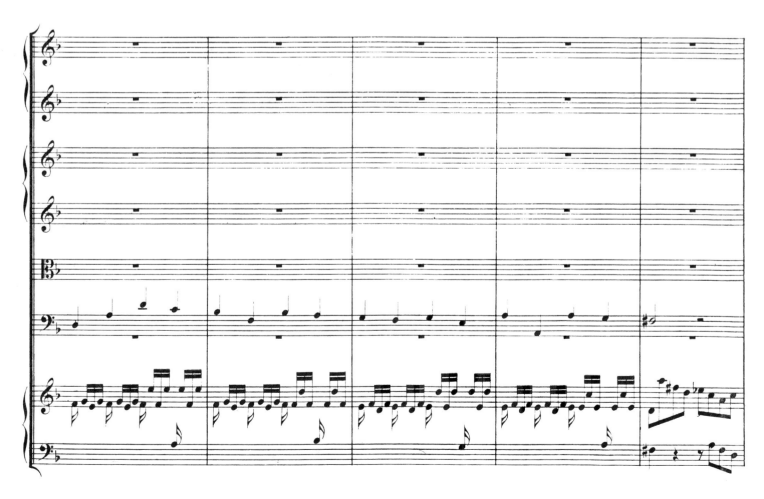

Concerto in G Minor (BWV 1058)

Allegro assai.